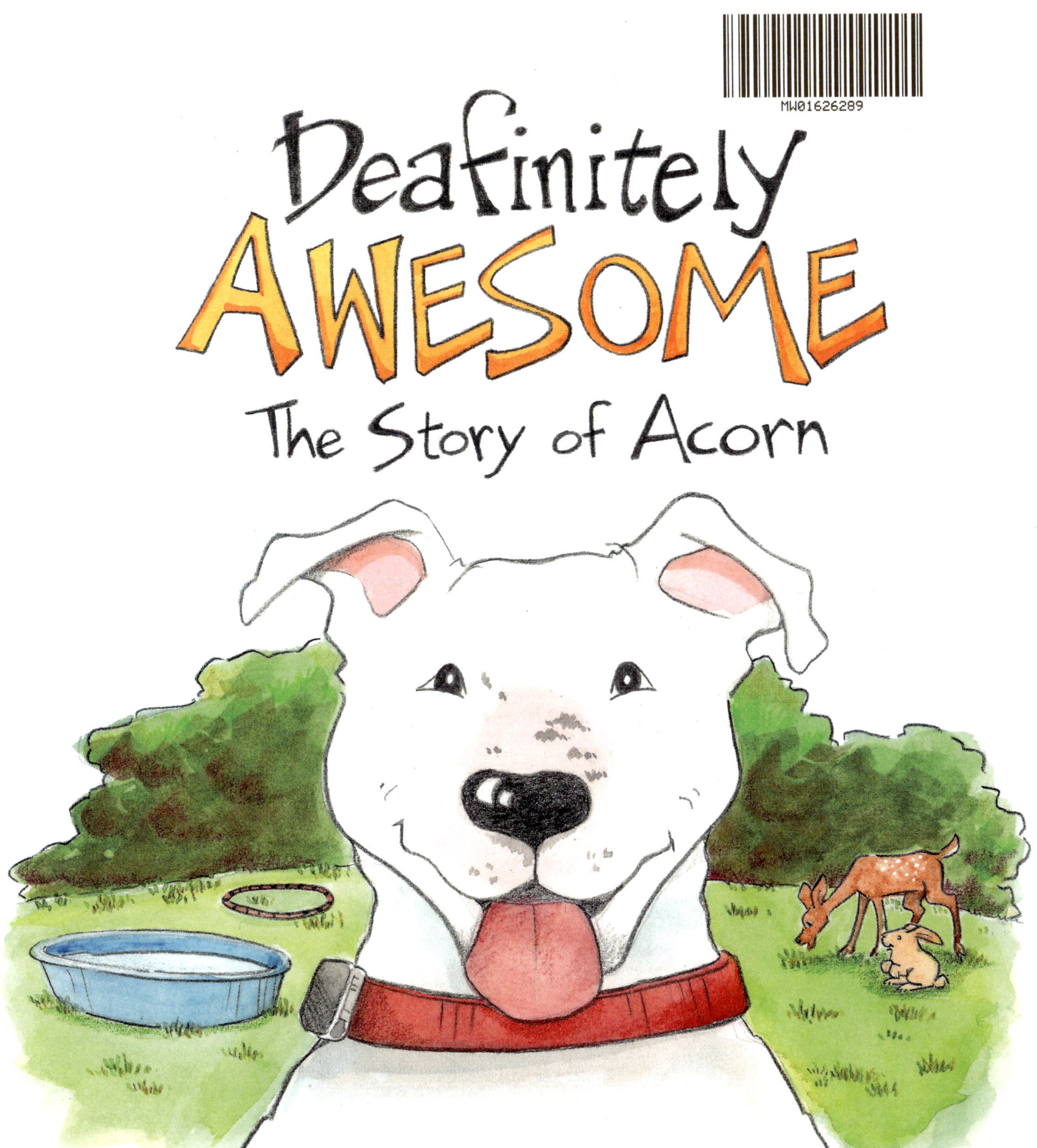


By Timy Sullivan as told by Mary L. Motley

Illustrated by Jenny Campbell

First edition February 2019

ISBN 978-1-7336685-0-7

# Acknowledgments

I will be forever grateful to Acorn's adopter Mary Motley for inviting me into their world. It has been an honor to tell the story of this truly awesome dog and his equally awesome "mom." Our thanks to Illustrator Jenny Campbell for so perfectly capturing Acorn's big personality in her drawings and to designer Heidi Wormser for bringing our book to life.

—Timy Sullivan

I would like to thank all those whose support and assistance proved to be invaluable in Acorn's journey from the "wild and crazy puppy who wouldn't listen" to a smart, attentive, charismatic and loving companion who has stolen the hearts of his many fans and become an ambassador for shelter dogs, deaf dogs, and pit bulls.

Special thanks go to the staff and volunteers at Cleveland Animal Care and Control (CACC) for giving me the opportunity to work with and ultimately adopt Acorn. I should clarify one thing. Yes — the City Kennel at the time *was* a very old building with small stacked cages and drains that made it impossible for the dogs to have toys. However, Acorn was given a bed. Unfortunately he turned it upside down and chewed off the legs. I guess that should have told me what I was getting into. Since this book was written, CACC has moved into a brand new state-of-the-art green building.

Many of the important lessons Acorn learned came through the CITY DOGS program, designed to change the image of the pit bull dogs who make up the majority of the kennel population. Acorn got to go on group runs and hikes with other kennel residents as a member of the CITY DOGS Runners. That's where he learned not to lunge at passing cars, joggers and bikers. Those outings gave me a chance to teach him to focus in a controlled but realistic environment. He also got to participate in the Dogs Playing for Life™ program (www.dogsplayingforlife.com), where he learned to speak DOG.

I'd also like to thank:

Camp Bow Wow

Cold Nose Companions and trainer Carol Peter

Deaf Dogs Rock

Friends of the Cleveland Kennel

Greg Murray Photography

Loehr Animal Behavior

Petco Foundation

...and finally, a special thanks to my family for their support.

—Mary Motley

It was a cold winter morning in the city. An icy wind blew drifts of snow across the frozen sidewalk. Men and women tucked their heads down into their collars like turtles as they hurried off to work.

Under a big green dumpster, a small white puppy lay shivering in a tight little ball trying his best to stay warm.

The puppy didn't know where he was or how he got there. He just knew he had once been warm and safe with a mom who loved him and brothers and sisters to play with.

Now he was alone and scared and hungry.

"I want my mom," he whimpered as he peeked out from his hiding place. "She's got to be around here somewhere. If I can just find my mom, I'll be warm and safe again."

And so the little white puppy crawled out from his hiding place and set out to find his mom.

He tried to follow the people who were scurrying down the sidewalk, but they were so big and they all moved so fast. It was hard not to get under their feet. They looked at him and moved their mouths in a strange way that made no sense to him. He was surrounded by people but he felt completely alone.

Finally a pretty little girl came toward him with outstretched arms and a happy mouth.

"She'll help me find my mom," the puppy thought as he dashed up to give her a friendly lick.

The little girl smiled sweetly and touched him softly on the head before a woman took her hand and gently pulled her across the street.

The puppy tried to follow but cars and big trucks flew by just missing him. Drivers leaned out of their windows, waving their arms and moving their mouths in that strange way he didn't understand.

Terrified, the puppy dashed back to the safety of the sidewalk. Afraid to move, he sat down and began to cry.

"I'll never find my mom," he sobbed, as a tear ran down his face and splashed on the frozen ground.

Just as he was about to give up, he opened one eye and saw feet in front of him. His first instinct was to run. But the feet, it turned out, were attached to a woman who was moving her mouth in a happy way and reaching out to him with something that smelled so good, it made his tummy rumble.

Quick as a wink, the woman scooped him up, wrapped him in a warm blanket, and put him in her car. As she drove, the tired little puppy munched happily on the treat she gave him. "I'll bet this is the person who will help me find my mom," he thought as he nodded off to sleep.

When the puppy woke up, he was in a room that smelled kind of funny and a woman with bright red hair was bent down next to him. She had a nice face but the first thing she did was poke him with something sharp.

“Hey,” he barked, “That hurt.”

The woman held him close and kissed him right on the top of his head.

Then she picked him up, looked him right in the eye and moved her mouth in that happy way.

The puppy didn't understand her words and, even if he had, he didn't know anything about acorns growing into giant oak trees. But at that moment, he felt safe and warm for the first time in a very long while.

Sadly, that good feeling didn't last long. The next thing he knew, the puppy was in a small concrete cage with bars on the front and a sign that read "Adopt Me. My Name is Acorn." He had no bed and he had no toys and, worst of all, he had no way to get out. He could smell that there were lots of other dogs around, but the only ones he could see did not look happy. It's true, he was no longer cold or hungry — but once again, Acorn was scared.

"Let me out," he barked. "I have to get out of here so I can find my mom." No one seemed to care.

And so Acorn did the only thing he could think of to get attention. He threw his water bowl, sending the contents splashing out into the aisle. Then he started banging the bowl against the bars of his cage — over and over and over again.

At first it seemed to work. A nice man came and took him out of his cage. He brought him outside where a bunch of other dogs were running around, playing hide and seek in tunnels and chasing each other up and down a slide.

Acorn was so happy to be out of that awful cage, he zoomed around and around in circles. The nice man just kept smiling at him. He didn't even mind when Acorn rolled in the mud and turned his white coat a dirty gray. The puppy was having so much fun, he almost forgot about finding his mom.

When he remembered, Acorn instantly stopped playing and ran for the gate. “This was fun,” he barked to the nice man, “but I need you to open up now so I can go find my mom.”

Unfortunately, The nice man didn't let him out to go find his mom. Instead he put Acorn back in his cage with a yummy treat and a pat on the head. He even refilled his water bowl.

But then he just walked away.

At first, Acorn was so sad, he just lay down on the hard concrete and whimpered. But then he remembered his mom and how much he missed her. He knew he had to find her so he went right back to doing the only thing he could think of to get someone to let him out of that cage.

Every time someone refilled his water bowl, Acorn threw it against the bars, soaking anyone who was walking by. Then he'd bang that bowl against the bars of his cage and bang it and bang it and bang it.

After a few days of this, a pretty young woman wearing a STAFF shirt asked a volunteer named Mary to take Acorn home for a few days to give everyone, including the bowl-banging puppy, a little break. "**He just won't listen**," the young woman said. "We are all at our wits' end."

Acorn had no idea what was going on, but he thought this woman just might be the one who could help him find his mom. So he stopped banging and gave her his best smile.

"How hard can this be?" Mary thought as she reached in to lift Acorn out of his cage.

She soon found out.

Acorn behaved horribly in the car, barking and ripping up the comfy blanket Mary had given him.

"They're right," she thought, "**this puppy just doesn't listen.**"

Home, it turned out, was a magical place with couches and chairs and rugs and all sorts of wonderful stuff Acorn had never seen before. He ran through the house jumping on all the furniture, throwing pillows around, grabbing books and pictures off tables and generally making a complete mess of the place.

No matter how many times Mary tried to get Acorn's attention, he just kept running around like a white tornado destroying everything in sight.

**He just wouldn't listen.**

Finally, when Acorn was all worn out, Mary managed to carry him into his own room with a nice soft bed in a comfy crate and a big bone to chew on. Acorn was so happy to be out of his awful cage that he slept through the night, dreaming about his mom.

The next morning, Mary went to check on her visitor. She called to him from outside his bedroom, but he didn't make a sound. Then she knocked on the bedroom door. Still nothing. He didn't even move when she opened the door to his crate and called his name again. Finally, she gently put her hand on his back. Acorn turned his head and, for the second time, gave her his perfect puppy smile.

That's when Mary understood something that would change both their lives.

**Acorn was Deaf!**

Acorn didn't **listen** because he couldn't **hear**.
In all his life, Acorn hadn't heard a single thing.

Not the people on the sidewalk.

Not the horns honking when he tried to cross the street.

Not the nice lady with the bright red hair giving him his name.

Not the other dogs barking in the kennel.

Not the annoying noise he made banging his water bowl against the bars.

Mary immediately took Acorn back to the kennel so he could be tested for deafness. It was true. Acorn had been born deaf and would never be able to hear.

When Mary got the news, she cried. She knew that in a kennel full of beautiful, healthy, hearing dogs needing homes, it would be very hard for an out-of-control deaf puppy to get a family to adopt him.

And so, Mary decided to take Acorn home with her … just until the right family could be found.

Mary was a teacher and she had trained dogs for many years, but she had no idea how to talk to a deaf dog.

That night, as Acorn lay at her feet, Mary started reading everything she could find on the subject. Finally, she looked over at the little white puppy who had suddenly entered her life and moved her mouth in that strange way that people seemed to do. Even though Acorn didn't hear the words, he saw her smile and somehow, he began to understand.

The very next day, Mary started teaching Acorn his new language. It was called sign language because she made signs with her hands to stand for words. The trick was finding a way to get this whirling dervish of a puppy to stand still and watch her hands.

Mary knew she could get Acorn to look at her by gently touching him and giving him the "watch me" sign by pointing to her eyes. Mary also knew Acorn loved hot dog slices almost more than anything. Now, the minute he looked at her, she gave him a "thumbs up" to let him know he had done something good, followed by a hot dog slice.

Each time Acorn looked right into her eyes, she gave him another "thumbs up" and a hot dog slice.

At first, Acorn had no idea what she was doing. He just knew he really liked those hot dogs and it seemed all he had to do to get one was look at Mary whenever she touched him and pointed to her eyes.

Finally one day, Acorn GOT it.

He figured out that  meant "watch me"

and he understood that Mary could "talk" to him with her hands.

He also understood that  meant "good job."

Acorn was so excited, he smiled from ear to ear and jumped up and down with delight. From that moment on, learning his new language was Acorn's very favorite thing to do.

Acorn wanted to learn everything. Within a couple of weeks, he was doing all the things a well-trained puppy does.

Mary signed "Sit" and he sat.

Mary signed "Down" and he lay down.

Mary signed "Stay" and he stayed perfectly still instead of running around the house making trouble.

He even learned signs for shake, roll over, turn in a circle, and jump through a hoop. He always knew he got it right when he saw that "thumbs up."

Mary's favorite thing was signing Acorn to "Come" and watching him run right to her, ears flapping and tail wagging.

Mary was so pleased with Acorn's progress that she decided to enroll him in Dog Obedience School to see how he'd do with hearing dogs. He was the youngest dog in class and the only one who couldn't hear, but that didn't make any difference to Acorn. He just did everything Mary's hands "told" him to do. He was the class star!

But there was one more language Acorn had to learn — and that was the language of DOG. Because he had grown up without a mom or brothers and sisters, he had never learned how dogs "talk" to each other.

When Mary took him to play with other dogs, Acorn sometimes got in trouble because he couldn't hear his playmates' barks and yelps and little growls warning him that he was playing too rough. Acorn just wanted to make friends, but the other dogs thought he was trying to start a fight and sometimes they even hurt him to make him stop.

Soon, however, Acorn figured out that dogs sign with their bodies just the way Mary signs with her hands. For example, he learned that ears flat back and bared teeth mean "back off, you're playing too rough."

Once Acorn learned the language of DOG, he made lots of doggie friends. Mary said he was the smartest dog in the world. She called him bilingual. That means he knows two languages — his special doggie sign language and DOG.

Now Acorn was ready to find his forever home.

Every weekend, Mary dressed him up in a fancy vest and took him to a local adoption event. "He's so cute," people said over and over again as Acorn showed off his skills, but they always added, "I wouldn't know how to handle a deaf dog."

Two nice families did take Acorn home, but they both brought him back in a couple of days because "**he wouldn't listen.**"

Mary welcomed him back with hugs and kisses.

But secretly, Mary was very worried that Acorn would never find the home he deserved.

One day, Mary had to go on a long trip for her work. She arranged for Acorn to stay in a top-notch doggie hotel while she was gone.

The caregivers at the doggie hotel fell in love with Acorn. They played with him and cuddled him. But no one knew his language and, although they kept moving their mouths in the way people do, Acorn had no idea what they were saying. Once again he was surrounded by people but all alone. He was miserable.

It turned out that Mary was miserable too. As she sat on the plane heading home, she realized that she and Acorn were meant to be together.

And right then, Mary made a big decision. "As soon as I get home," she thought, "I'm going to adopt Acorn."

And that is what she did.

Since that day, Acorn and Mary have been a team sharing what they have learned together to help other deaf dogs find their forever homes.

Of course, it isn't all work and no play for Acorn. He no longer tears the house apart, but he is still full of mischief. Because he is so good at watching Mary, he has learned a lot more than his signs. In fact, he's started copying everything Mary does.

Mary has learned she has to watch Acorn as much as Acorn has to watch her.

…especially when there is water around.

He learned how to turn on the bathtub faucet and hop right in whenever he wants a bath.

And to drag his baby pool out from under the deck when he wants a swim.

He also loves puddles. The really muddy ones are the best.

But Acorn hates water when it's falling from the sky. He thinks going out in the rain will make him melt.

Actually, Acorn pretty much loves everyone and everything. He loves meeting children and other dogs on his long walks with Mary. He welcomes the deer and rabbits that wander into in his back yard and he enjoys just lying quietly on his back on the picnic table and watching the clouds go by.

Mary thinks everything Acorn does is just wonderful.
She especially loves his sense of humor.

Sometimes, when Acorn knows he's doing something wrong, like trying to steal cookies off the counter while Mary is signing him "No," he turns his back so he can't see her hands.

Mary just laughs and kisses him and tells him over and over again how much she loves him.

And even though he still can't hear the words, he *deafinitely* understands that his long search is over.

ACORN HAS FOUND HIS MOM!

## Epilogue

You might think that's the end of the story. But it's just the beginning.

Acorn was the first known deaf dog adopted from Cleveland Animal Care and Control, but he was not the last. Mary has become an advocate for the deaf dogs who end up at the kennel and a mentor for other adopters who step up to bring dogs like Acorn into their families. Acorn has become famous all over the country thanks to his very own Facebook page "Deafinitely Awesome – the Adventures of Acorn." He's won generous Petco Foundation grants for the kennel and appeared in the Petco Foundation 2019 calendar (available at www.petcofoundation.org), as well as noted animal photographer Greg Murray's 2019 Pit Bull Heroes calendar (available at www.gmurrayphoto.com). His portrait even appears on a wine bottle.

When he's not making mischief at home with his mom, he spends his days showing the world that deafness is not a limitation — that a deaf dog can do anything a hearing dog can do.

Photo: Steve Springer

## A final word from Mary

The first time Acorn looked into my eyes and smiled after I signed, "Watch me," I knew he understood that my hands and his eyes connected us. At that moment both our lives changed forever. We are bonded in a very special way and our mission is to be ambassadors for the deaf, both human and animal. I've trained dogs for years, and the truth is, deaf dogs like Acorn are often easier to train than hearing dogs because they are so completely focused on their people and are not easily distracted. Because they are not afraid of thunderstorms, fireworks, honking horns or other loud noises, they can become great therapy dogs.

Acorn knows more than 30 hand signals and is learning more every day. I have never worried about his ability to learn. The challenge for me has been thinking up new things to teach him.

With his movie star looks and wicked sense of humor, Acorn proves every day that being deaf is not a limitation, that shelter dogs make wonderful family pets, and that pit bulls are just dogs with big heads.

It is my hope that one day deaf dogs will be welcomed into homes as dogs that are not very different from hearing dogs. They just "listen with their eyes and hear with their hearts."

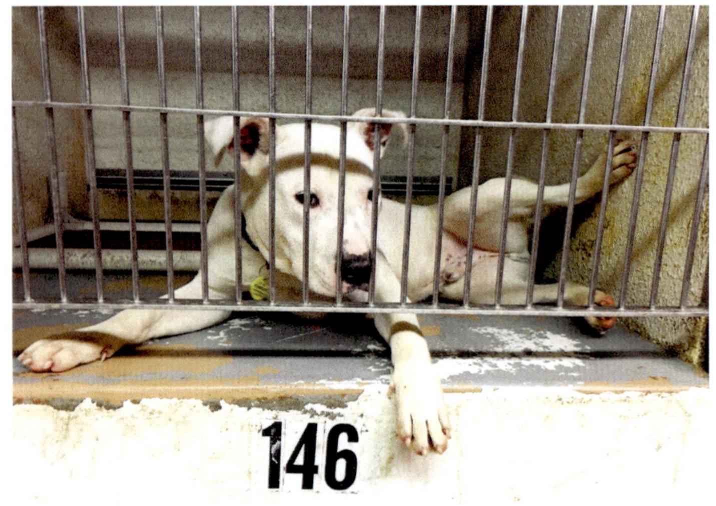

Photo: Greg Murray

Photo: Greg Murray

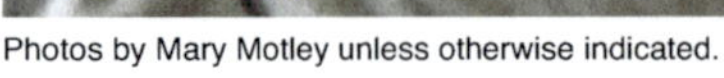
Photos by Mary Motley unless otherwise indicated.

Made in the USA
Columbia, SC
27 March 2019